PowerPoint 2007
Foundation to Intermediate Guide

D1513398

Chris Voyse and Patrice Muse

Published by
Voyse Recognition Limited

September 2007

861756

First Published in Great Britain in 2007

Voyse Recognition Limited
Century Business Centre
Manvers Way
Manvers
Rotherham
South Yorkshire
S63 5DA
01709 300188

ISBN 978-1-905657-24-7

Foundation to Intermediate Level Objectives

- Introduction to PowerPoint

- Methodology of Creating Presentations

- Bullets and Numbering Features

- Creating, Opening and Saving a Presentation

- Creating Header and Footer Options

- Working with Shapes, Clip Art and Text

- Using the Undo and Redo Feature

- Using the Spell Check Feature

- Working with the Slide Master

- Setting Colour Schemes

- Working with Placeholders

- The Creation of Charts

- Using the Outline View

- Using the Slide Sorter View

- Working with Graphics

- Inserting Objects

- Chart Layout View

- Running a Slide Show

- Hide and Unhide Slides

- Setting Timings and Transitions

- Shortcut Keys

Table of Contents

Introducing the PowerPoint Screen

PowerPoint 2007 is an application that enables slides to be generated, edited and presented to either an individual or group of users. Notes pages can be generated to enhance the presentation, handouts can be produced and PowerPoint offers a variety of printing options.

Opening PowerPoint

There are several ways that this application can be opened. To open the PowerPoint 2007 application, select the Start Button [image], move the mouse pointer [image] and pause over ▸ **All Programs** , click with the left [image] button on 📄 **Microsoft Office** ; select 🔲 **Microsoft Office PowerPoint 2007** , click with the left [image] button to open the programme.

Tour of the Screen

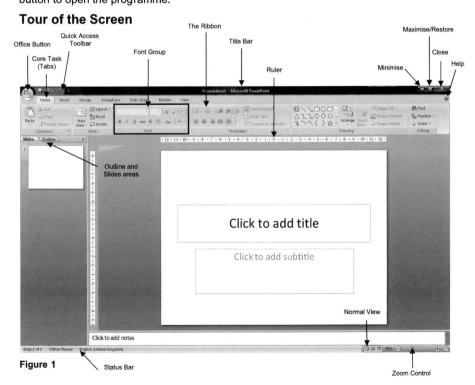

Figure 1   Status Bar

Office Button

In PowerPoint 2007 the Office Button 🖱 replaces the file menu found in previous versions of PowerPoint and displays the commands for Open, New, Save, Save As, Print, Prepare, Send, Publish, Business Contact Manager and Close and the related options available under each command.

Quick Access Toolbar

The Quick Access Toolbar can be found in the top section of the screen. It allows the user to display commands that are regularly used and that are independent of their associated tabs. There is the option to locate the Quick Access Toolbar in two locations near to the top section of the screen.

Title Bar

The Title Bar is highlighted in black and defines the name of the application that you are in and the name of the presentation you have opened. PowerPoint will automatically display the default name, for example Presentation1, however, once the presentation has been saved the name of the saved presentation will be displayed in this area.

The Ribbon

The Ribbon is new to PowerPoint 2007 and is the control centre to quickly help you find the commands that help you to complete a task. The Ribbon is organised into three parts

1. **Core Tasks**: consisting of seven Tabs

   Home, Insert, Design, Animations, Slide Show, Review and View

2. **Groups**: related items grouped together

3. **Commands**: buttons, boxes and menus that give instruction

The Ribbon organises the commands into logical groups all collected together under the Tabs with each Tab relating to a type of activity. Some Tabs only appear when they are needed whilst others are visible all the time.

To minimise the Ribbon double click with the left 🖱 button on the active Tab, for example `Design`, the Ribbon and its commands disappear. To display the Ribbon and its commands, click with the left 🖱 button on the Tab. Alternatively press `Ctrl` `F1` to collapse or expand the Tabs.

Help Icon

The Help ⓘ icon can be found on the Ribbon or by pressing `F1`.

Scroll Bars

Horizontal and Vertical scroll bars enable users to move around the presentation.

Zoom Control

To use the Zoom Control drag with the left 🖱 button to increase (magnify) or decrease the presentation to display the information larger or smaller on the screen.

Status Bar

The Status Bar is at the bottom of the screen, to customise the Status Bar

1. Right 🖱 click on the Status Bar, the Customise Status Bar appears

2. To activate the View Indicator to be displayed in the Status Bar

3. Click with the left 🖱 button on ⌑ View Indicator

4. A tick ✓ is displayed to indicate the feature has been activated

5. Click back in the presentation

6. Slide 1 of 1 is displayed in the Status Bar to show that the View Indicated is activated

The Status Bar also tells the user which theme as been applied to the selected slide "Office Theme"

Notes Page

Notes Page displays a reduced image of the slide, it also allows the user to edit any notes before printing them out.

Normal View

The Normal View icon ▣ is on the left hand side of the Status Bar or is activated by

selecting View , Normal from the Ribbon.

Slide Sorter View

The Sorter View icon ▦ is found on the Status Bar or is activated by selecting View ,

Slide Sorter from the Ribbon. This displays all the slides within a presentation. Slides can be moved or copied and slide transition effects displayed and added from here for an onscreen slide show.

Slide Show

The Slide Show can be displayed by selecting the Slide Show icon 🖵 that is located on

the Status Bar or is activated by selecting View , Slide Show from the Ribbon.

Note: If you are working in Windows XP instead of Windows Vista, dialog boxes may look different but function in a similar way.

Methodology of Creating Presentations

A presentation is a means of communicating information to an audience in a clear and effective manner using a variety of output media.

Preparation Work before Creating a Presentation

How will the presentation be delivered to the audience?

- With a computer using a projector
- On a standalone computer
- Simple slide show
- Stand up presentation
- Use of acetates or an overhead projector
- Use of handouts
- Do corporate colours and font styles need to be included in the presentation?
- What graphics are to be used in the presentation?
- Does the presentation require use of transitions?
- Are Header and Footer areas required?
- What type of Background is required?

Page Setup

PowerPoint displays the default design for a title slide; however this can be changed by using Page Setup.

1. Select Design , Page Setup

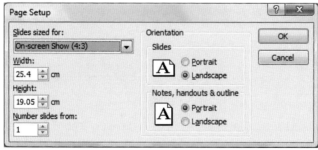

Figure 2

2. In the **S**lides sized for: area, the default is set as On-screen Show
3. Choose the ▼ to view alternative options
4. Choose the orientation settings for Slides and Notes, handouts and outline
5. Press OK

Figure 3

1. PowerPoint contains 12 themes available from the Themes grouping
2. The Themes grouping contains built in [Colors ▾], [A Fonts ▾] and [Effects ▾]

Defining the Background Colour

The type of presentation will determine the choice of background.

1. Select the [Design] Tab, click with the left ⌁ button on [Background Styles ▾]
2. The following gallery appears

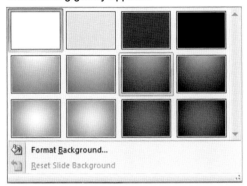

Figure 4

3. Move over any of the styles to display the theme colours in the presentation
4. Click with the left ⌁ button on [Format Background...]
5. The Format Background dialog box is displayed

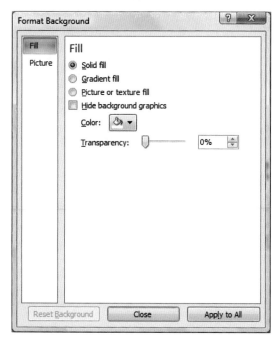

Figure 5

6. Select the **C**olour icon 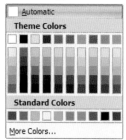 to expand the menu

Figure 6

7. Select a Theme Colour, the slide changes to show the chosen colour

8. Press [Format Background...] , choose [Reset Slide Background]

9. The slide changes back to the default slide colour

10. Click with the left button on [Format Background...]

11. Select the **C**olour icon , choose [More Colors...]

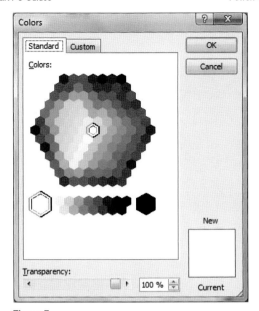

Figure 7

12. The Standard colours are displayed, select the [Custom] Tab

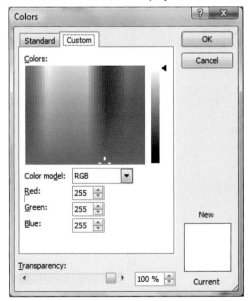

Figure 8

13. Select a colour of your choice to be used in the presentation

14. To lighten or darken the colour use the black marker ◀

15. Select [OK]

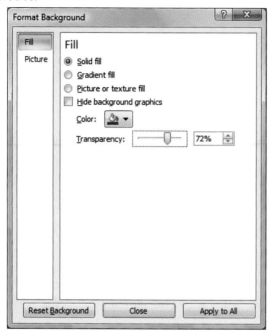

Figure 9

16. Select **T**ransparency, adjust the transparency to 72%

17. Press [Apply to All]

18. The background colour is applied to all the slides in the presentation

Fill Effects

1. Choose | Design |, select | Background Styles ▾ |, choose | Format Background... |
2. The Format Background dialog box appears

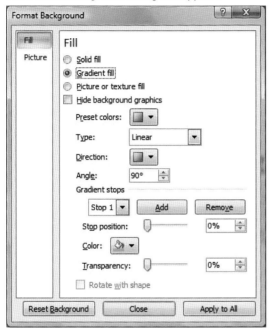

Figure 10

3. Click on the **G**radient fill, select | Preset colors: ▾ |
4. The P**r**eset colour pallet is displayed

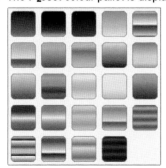

Figure 11

5. Select a colour, choose , select a shading style

Figure 12

6. The options change with each shading style

7. In the Gradient stops box adjust the Stop position to 40%, press [Add]

Figure 13

8. Add a second and third stop

9. Select [Apply to All], click [Close]

10. The fill effect is applied to all the slides in the presentation

Picture and Texture Effects

1. Choose [Design], select [Background Styles ▾], choose [Format Background...]

2. The Format Background dialog box appears

3. Press with the left button on [◉ Picture or texture fill]

Figure 14

4. Select the Texture icon, choose Purple Mesh

5. Use the [Transparency: ——◯——— 55% ▲▼] slide ruler to adjust the texture

6. Alternatively, click [File...] to move to the Sample Pictures area

7. Select the file name Tree, choose [Insert ▼]

8. Choose [Clip Art...] to select a piece of clipart as a background

9. [Apply to All] applies the picture or textured effect to all the slides

10. Select [Close]

Using the Bullets and Numbering Feature

PowerPoint can create text to appear on different levels using different font styles and colours.

1. Select , choose

2. In the Click to add title area type: Using Bullets

3. In the Click to add text area type: Level 1, press [Enter] to move to the next bullet

4. To indent the bullet and text to the next level, select Increase Indent from the Paragraph Grouping

5. Type Level 2

6. Repeat steps 5 and 6, type Level 3

7. Continue the process until you have generated five levels

8. To move back a level, click the left button on the level to be changed

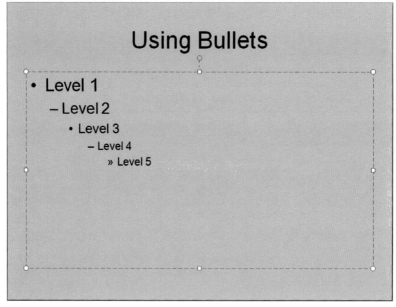

Figure 15

9. Select the Decrease Indent icon to move back to the required level

Formatting Bullets

1. Select the bullet(s) to be formatted
2. Click on the downward pointing arrow on the Bullets icon ⊞▾ from the Paragraph Grouping

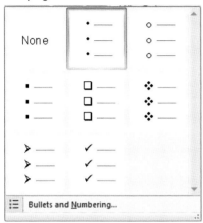

Figure 16

3. Select ⠿ Bullets and Numbering...
4. The Bullets and Numbering dialog box appears

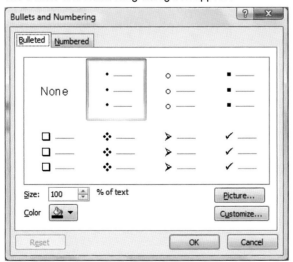

Figure 17

5. Adjust the size as required Size: [100] % of text

6. Choose Color [🎨 ▾] to define the required colour

7. Click [Customize...], select the font Wingdings

8. Use the scroll bars to view the different bullet styles

9. Select a graphical style required for the bullet

10. Press [OK] twice to return the presentation

11. The selected bullet style is applied

12. Select [View], [☑ Ruler] to display the ruler [ruler icon]

13. Press [Alt] [W] [R] to show or hide the ruler

14. The ⌂ icon is used to increase the distanced from the bullet

15. The ▽ icon enables the bullet to be moved nearer to the text

16. To move bullet and text together, click and drag the left 🖱 button on the ▭ icon

Saving a Presentation

1. Select

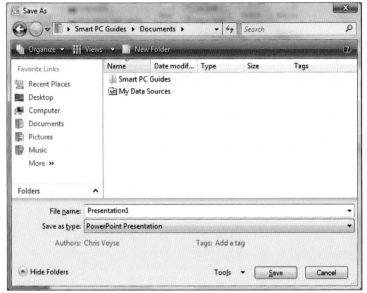

Figure 18

2. Alternatively press F12 to display the Save As dialog box

3. In the File name area save the presentation as Using Bullets

4. In the Save as type area the default is set to save items as a PowerPoint Presentation

5. Select Save

6. The title bar area displays the named presentation

Note: If a user requires to save, open or work in a presentation in a previous version, click on the downward arrow in the Save as type dialog box and select, PowerPoint 97-2003 Presentation, click Save. The Compatibility Checker may appear if features in 2007 have been used that are not available in previous versions. In 2007 the Title bar will state [Compatibility Mode] identifying that the presentation is not saved in a 2007 format.

To Add a New Slide to a Presentation

1. Select Home

2. Click on the downward pointing arrow on the New Slide icon

3. Alternatively press Alt H I

4. Choose the required layout

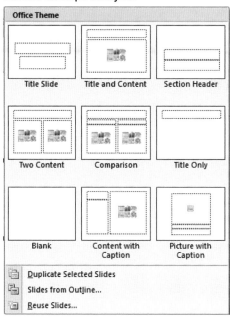

Figure 19

5. To change the layout of the slide, re-select the slide

6. Choose Layout and select the new layout

Creating Header and Footer Options

1. Select Insert , Header & Footer, the Header and Footer dialog box appears

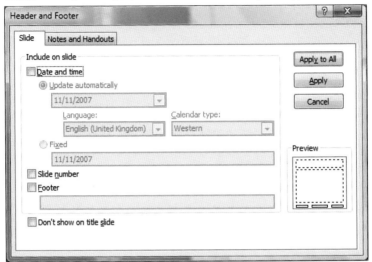

Figure 20

2. Select **D**ate and time, choose **U**pdate automatically

Figure 21

3. Or select Fi**x**ed, type in the date required

4. Tick ☑ Slide number to identify a slide by a number

5. Click in the **F**ooter area, type the required information

6. Apply to All applies the Header and Footer information to all the Slides

7. Apply inserts the information to an individual slide

8. Select ☑ Don't show on title slide if information is not to be displayed

Exercise 1: - Create a Simple Presentation

1. Open a new presentation
2. In the Click to add title, type Working with PowerPoint
3. In the Click to add subtitle, type your name
4. Add a coloured background or texture of your choice

Two Content

5. Add the new slide named
6. Ensure the ruler is displayed, create the following slide

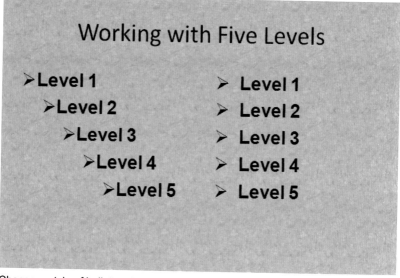

7. Choose a style of bullet and display the five levels in the left column
8. Highlight the five levels, change the font size to 32
9. In the right column display five bullets at Level 1
10. In the right column click on the ▽ triangle and drag to 2
11. Use the ruler marker triangle 🔺 to increase the spacing from the bullet
12. Add a new slide Title Only, add the title Working with Shapes
13. Save the presentation as Creating My First Presentation
14. Close the presentation

Working with Shapes, Clip Art and Text

Blank

1. Open a new presentation, select

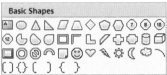

2. Select Insert , Shapes , choose Basic Shapes, click on a shape to select it

Figure 22

3. Move the mouse pointer onto the blank slide

4. Click and drag with the left button to insert the shape

5. Repeat the process to add three additional shapes

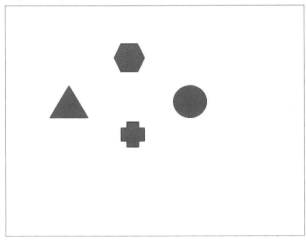

Figure 23

6. Click and drag the shapes to move them to different locations on the slide

Change AutoShape Default Colour

1. Double click on the select shape with the right 🖰 button
2. Select 📝 Format Shape...
3. The Format Shape dialog box appears

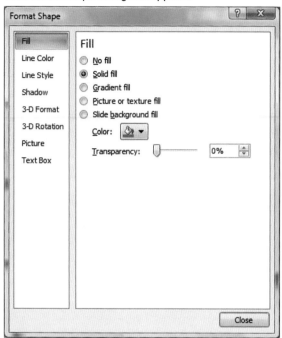

Figure 24

4. To change the fill colour select ⦿ Solid fill , Color: 🎨 ▾
5. To lighten or darken a selected colour, adjust Transparency to the required shade

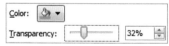

Figure 25

6. To change the colour and weight of lines select Line Color
7. To change the line style select Line Style , choose the required options

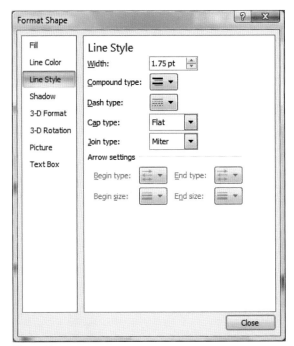

Figure 26

8. Choose [Close] to view the changes to the slide

9. Save the changes

Set AutoShape Defaults

1. Move the mouse pointer ⬚ over the shape with the new default settings

2. Click with the right ⬚ button on the shape, choose [Set as Default Shape]

3. Select a shape from the basic shapes gallery

4. Click the left ⬚ button to display the shape with the new default settings

5. To revert to the original default setting

6. Move the mouse pointer ⬚ over the shape, double click with the right ⬚ button

7. Select [🖉 Format Shape...]

8. Choose the original settings, click [Close]

9. Move the mouse pointer ⬚ over the shape with the new default settings

10. Click with the right ⬚ button on the shape, choose [Set as Default Shape]

Using the Undo and Redo Feature

PowerPoint enables a user to enter text in a presentation and store that information in its memory allowing the user to go backwards or forwards on a step by step basis. The Undo 🔄 and Redo ↪ icons can be found on the Quick Access Toolbar located at the top of the screen.

To Amend the Undo Default Settings

1. Select 🅑, 🅑 PowerPoint Options, Advanced,

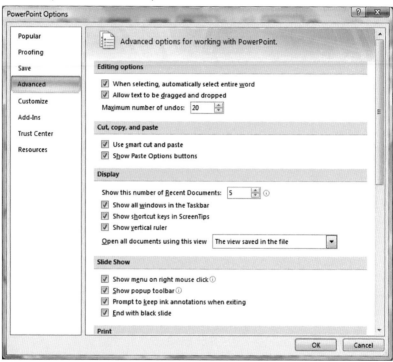

Figure 27

2. Select Editing options
3. Change the Ma**x**imum number of undo's to 150

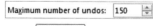

4. Press OK

Using Gridlines

When using drawing objects, gridlines can be switched on to help with accurate positioning of an object.

1. Select [View], [☑ Gridlines], alternatively press [Alt] [V] [I]

2. The Grid and Guides dialog box appears

Figure 28

3. Choose [☑ Snap objects to grid] and [☑ Display grid on screen]

4. Click [OK]

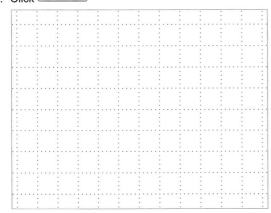

Figure 29

5. Grid lines appear on the slide in the screen as vertical and horizontal lines

6. Select [Alt] [V] [I], deselect the required tick to switch off the gridlines

7. Press [OK] to return to the presentation

Using the Spell Check Facility

1. Select , alternatively press F7
2. The Spell Checker will spell check the presentation or selected text
3. Words that are not recognised in the dictionary are highlighted

Figure 30

4. The dialog box highlights any applicable suggestions, select Ignore or Change

5. Add adds the word to the dictionary

6. Choose Ignore All to ignore all suggestions from the spell checker

7. Select Change All to change all corrections suggested from the spell checker

Working with the Slide Master

With the Slide Master a theme can be set for a presentation using font styles, background colours and company logos. Once created the attributes from the Slide Master are applied to the new slide, if selected the Slide Master incorporates the same identity to all the slides saving development time. If a date and time is applied for example, the Slide Master uses these settings for the entire presentation.

View Slide Master

1. Select View , Slide Master , or press Alt W M
2. This displays the Master Title style
3. Alternatively move the mouse pointer ⟨⟩ over Normal View ▦
4. Hold down the Shift key, double click with the left ⟨⟩ button
5. The following screen appears

Figure 31

To Change the Default Date and Time Setting

1. Highlight the date/time, select [Insert],

2. Select the required format

3. Choose [Default...]

4. The following prompt appears

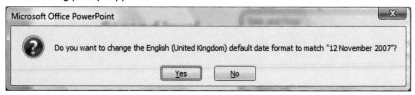

Figure 32

5. Click [Yes]

6. Press [OK] to apply the format to the presentation

Inserting Date and Time

1. Click on the Date placeholder in the bottom left hand corner of the Slide Master

2. Select  ,

3. The Header and Footer dialog box appears

4. Click with the left ⌕ button in the **D**ate and time, a tick ☑ is displayed

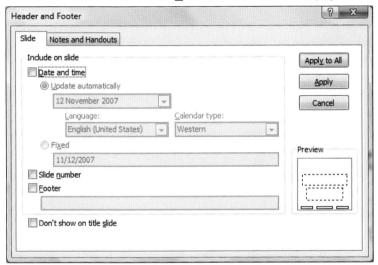

Figure 33

5. The **D**ate and time facility provides a variety of different formats

6. To update the date automatically, click ⊙ Update automatically

7. Alternatively choose the required format, click Apply to All

8. This will apply the formats to all the slides including any new slides added

9. To change the font colour or size of the of the date

10. Highlight the date, select Home

11. Click on the downward pointing arrow on the Font Colour icon **A** ▾

12. Select the required colour from the Theme Colours pallet

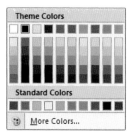

Figure 34

13. Alternatively select More Colours to define a more specific colour

14. Choose a Standard or Custom colour

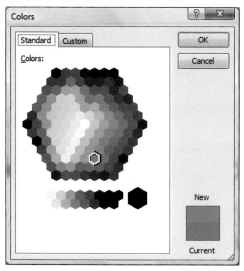

Figure 35

15. Press [OK] to apply the colour in the presentation

To Amend Data using the Footer Area

Slide Master allows the user to change the colour, size and style of data used.

1. Click in the footer area

2. Add a company or organisational name

3. If required amend the colour, style and size of the text

To Add a Background Picture

1. Select   Slide Master , Background Styles ▾ , Format Background...

2. The Format Background dialog box appears

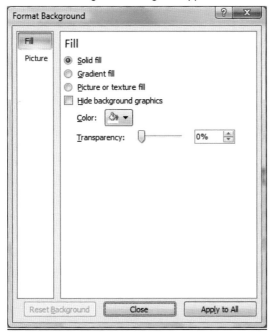

Figure 36

3. Click on ◉ Picture or texture fill

4. Select File...

5. Choose the required picture, click Insert ▾

6. Choose Apply to All to add the background to all the slides, or

7. Select Close to apply the background to the current slide

8. Selecting Reset Slide Background resets the background back to white

Setting Colour Schemes

A user can apply a different colour scheme to each individual slide in a presentation however, by editing or selecting a scheme the Master automatically applies the settings to every slide in the presentation.

1. Open a new presentation, select

2. Choose  from the Edit Theme Grouping

3. The All Themes gallery appears

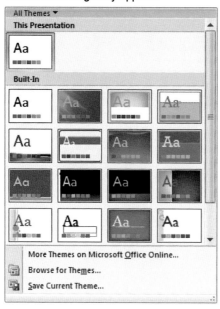

Figure 37

4. Select a theme from the Built-In gallery

5. Click on Colors

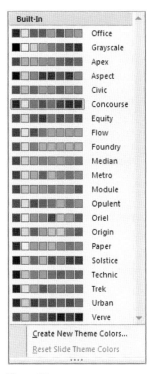

Figure 38

6. Choose the colour theme required

7. Alternatively select [<u>C</u>reate New Theme Colors...]

8. The Create New Theme Colours dialog box appears

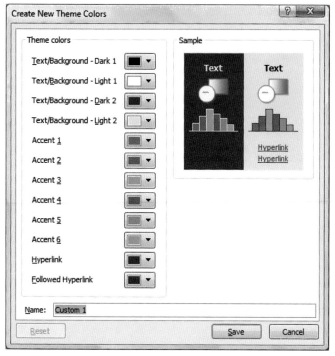

Figure 39

9. Choose the required colours for the pallet, press [Save]

Placeholders

When working in the Slide Master, Handout Master and Notes Master, placeholders appear in the four corners of the slide, these are named the Header Area, Date Area, Footer Area and Number Area. Think of a placeholder as a named text box, placeholders can be moved to another area or deleted.

To View the Handout Master Placeholders

1. Select  View ,  Handout Master , the following view is displayed

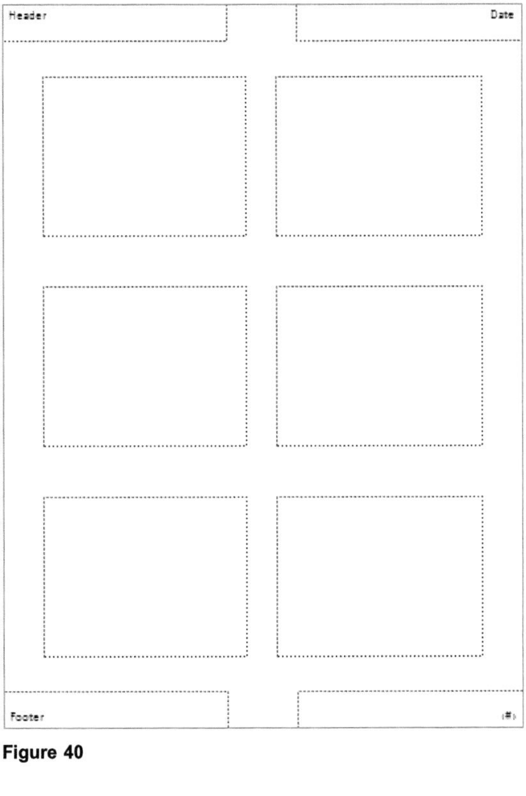

Figure 40

2. Alternatively select Insert, Header & Footer

3. The Header and Footer dialog box appears

4. Select the Notes and Handouts Tab

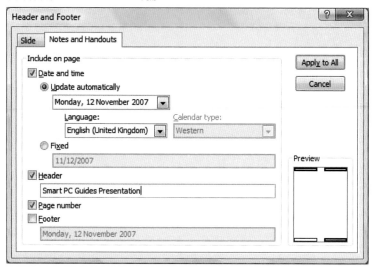

Figure 41

5. Select the required options, press Apply to All

6. Choose 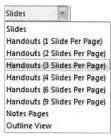, Print, Print Preview Preview and make changes to pages before printing.

7. Click on the downward pointing arrow on slides to expand the menu

Slides
Slides
Handouts (1 Slide Per Page)
Handouts (2 Slides Per Page)
Handouts (3 Slides Per Page)
Handouts (4 Slides Per Page)
Handouts (6 Slides Per Page)
Handouts (9 Slides Per Page)
Notes Pages
Outline View

Figure 42

8. Choose the handout option required

9. Alternatively click View , Handout Master to display the handout options

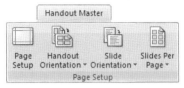

Figure 43

10. Select Slides Per Page ▾ , click on the required option

Figure 44

11. Choose Close Master View to return to the presentations Normal View

To Delete a Placeholder

1. Select  View , Handout Master

2. Remove the ticks from the placeholders not required

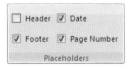

Figure 45

3. Choose Close Master View to return to the presentation

4. The placeholder is deleted from the master

To Move a Placeholder to a New Location

1. Click with the left  button on the header area in the placeholder
2. The Placeholder is selected

Figure 46

3. Hold the [Ctrl] key down, press the appropriate arrow ⬇ ⬆ ➡ ⬅ keys
4. The placeholder moves to the new destination

To Retrieve a Placeholder

1. If the handout master is not already displayed

2. Choose
3. Click inside the Handout Master
4. Press the right  button, select ▦ Handout Master Layout...

Figure 47

5. The placeholders in the active master are highlighted by a tick ☑
6. Click with the left ⬥ button to display the ☑ Date placeholder
7. Press [OK]
8. The date placeholder appears in the default position

Exercise 2: - Creating a Handout Master

1. Open Creating My First Presentation

2. Display the Handout Master by choosing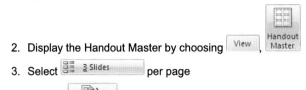

3. Select  per page

4. Choose 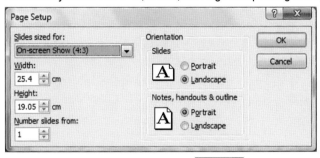, change the Orientation to

5. Alternatively select [Design], [Page Setup], the Page Setup dialog box appears

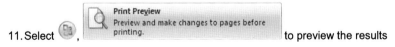

6. Set the Orientation to Landscape, click [OK]

7. Apply a handout background colour of your choice

8. Click in the Header, type Presentation Handout

9. Click in the Footer, type ABC Limited

10. Close Master View

11. Select ⓐ, Print Preview — Preview and make changes to pages before printing. to preview the results

12. Choose Slides , choose Handouts (3 Slides Per Page)

13. The result is displayed below

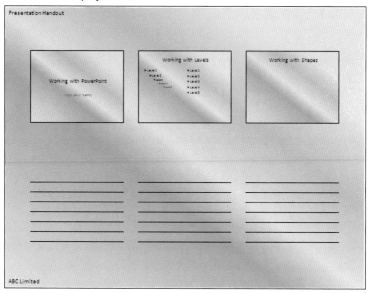

14. Save the presentation

Using SmartArt to Create an Organisational Chart

SmartArt allows users to create organisational charts using a variety of shapes. This is useful if a hieratical structure is required.

1. Open a new presentation, select the Title Only slide

2. Click in the title area of the slide, type My Organisational Chart

3. Select  the SmartArt Graphic dialog box appears

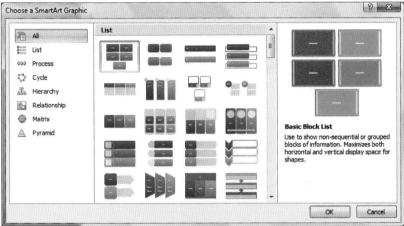

Figure 48

4. Select the category

5. Choose Organisational Chart, press [OK]

6. The organisational chart is displayed in the slide

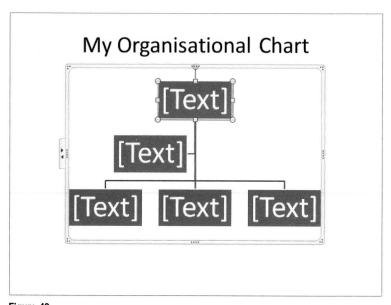

Figure 49

7. Click on the outer edge of the second text box, press Delete

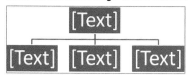

Figure 50

8. Click in the middle text box, press Delete

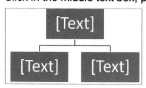

Figure 51

9. Click in the left hand side text box, choose Design from SmartArt Tools

10. Select Add Shape ▾, choose ⬚ Add Assistant

11. Repeat steps 9 and 10 to create a second text box

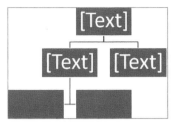

Figure 52

12. Click back in the first text box, type Managing Director

13. The text box will adjust to the appropriate size

14. Alternatively click the left button on the arrow on the outline area

15. The following dialog box appears

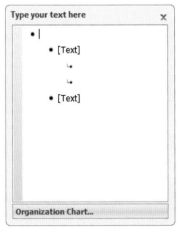

Figure 53

16. Type the text Managing Director, the text box automatically resizes

17. Press the downward arrow key to highlight the next text box

To Customise the Organisational Chart

1. Click in the Managing Director text box

2. Select to expand the colour gallery

3. Choose a colour of your choice

4. Click on the downward pointing arrow of the SmartArt Styles commands

Figure 54

5. Select 3-D Powder

6. Click in a text box, choose **Format** from **SmartArt Tools**

7. Click on the downward pointing arrow of WordArt Styles

Figure 55

8. Choose Gradient Fill - Accent 4, Reflection

9. To change the colour of the text, select **A Text Fill ▾**

10. Select **A Text Effects ▾** to apply a visual effect to the text

11. **✎ Text Outline ▾** changes the colour, width and line style

12. Click on **☞ Change Shape ▾** to change the shape of the text box

13. Save the presentation as My First Organisational Chart

Exercise 3: - Creating a Organisational Chart

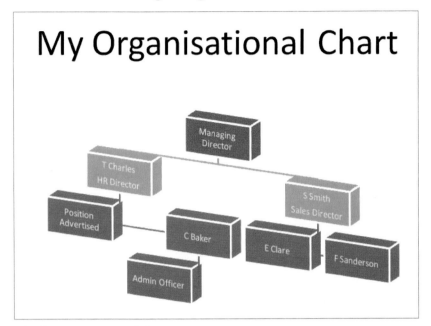

1. Open a new presentation
2. Create an Organisational Chart displaying four levels as shown above
3. Experiment using 3 different styles and colours from the gallery options
4. Apply a style of your choice and save to update the presentation

Using Outline View

The Outline View is a fast and easy way to create a quick outline for a presentation.

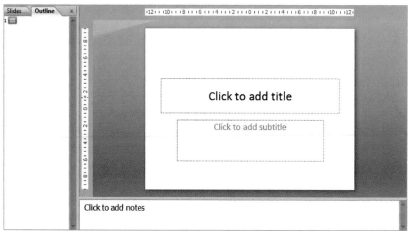

Figure 56

1. Open a new presentation
2. Select the Outline Tab ⟨Slides⟩ ⟨Outline⟩
3. Click with the left button after the icon 1
4. A flashing cursor is displayed
5. Type Smart PC Guides, the text is inserted into the title slide
6. Press Enter followed by the Tab key, type your name
7. The text appears in the Subtitle area
8. Press Enter, hold down the Shift key, press Tab
9. The flashing cursor goes back a level, slide 2 appears
10. Type the heading for the next slide, press Enter
11. Press Tab a bullet appears
12. Type the required list or select the Layout Tab to apply the required style

Exercise 4: - Working with Outline

The object of this exercise is to create a quick outline for a presentation. If some of the slides need to have a different layout, the layout changes when the appropriate option is selected.

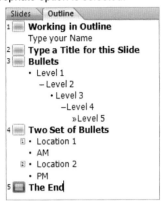

1. Working in Outline View to the left of the screen, type Working in Outline

2. The text appears in the slide and in the outline area

3. Press Enter

4. Press Tab , type your first name and surname

5. Slide 1 is complete

6. Press Enter , hold down Shift , press Tab , slide 2 text layout appears

7. Insert Type a Title for this Slide

8. Slide 2 is complete

9. Complete the text as displayed above for slide 3

10. Select Home , Layout ▾

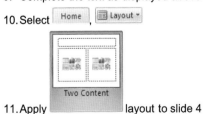

11. Apply   layout to slide 4

12. Type the following text

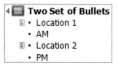

13. To move to column 2, press ⌈Ctrl⌉ and ⌈Enter⌉

14. Complete slide 5

15. Press ⌈Ctrl⌉ and the Home key to return to the beginning of the presentation

16. Click on the ⌈Slide Show⌉ Tab, use the ⌈↓⌉ key to run through the slides

17. Select ⌈Ctrl⌉ ⌈A⌉ to highlight all the slides in the presentation

18. Move the mouse pointer anywhere over the highlighted area in Outline

19. To collapse the slides, click with the right button, choose ⌈— Collapse ►⌉

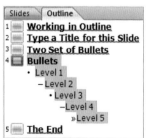

20. To move a slide, collapse the slide, click with the left button on the slide named Bullets

21. Place the slide Bullets in the new position as Slide 4

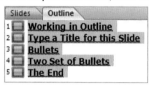

22. Choose the slide named Bullets, right click, press ⌈✚ Expand ►⌉

23. The text contents have moved, save the presentation as Working in Outline

Using Slide Sorter View

The Slide Sorter View provides an overall view of all the slides in the presentation and allows slides to be added, repositioned or deleted, as well as displaying transitions, animation effects and timings.

Moving Slides in the Slide Sorter View

1. Select

2. Click with the left 🖱 button on the slide to be moved

3. A orange border appears around each selected slide

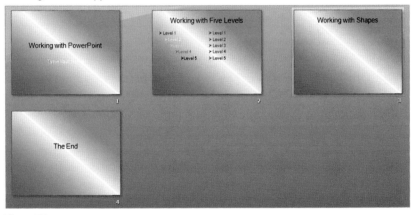

Figure 57

4. Click and hold the left 🖱 button down, drag the slide to its new location

5. A orange vertical line indicates where the slide will be moved to

6. When the left 🖱 button is released the slide is moved to the new location

Deleting Slides

1. Click with the left 🖱 button to select the slide to be deleted

2. Press the Delete key on the keyboard

Working with Graphics

Presentations can be enhanced and made more interesting by inserting graphics, drawing objects, pictures, charts or text and then by grouping, scaling, cropping or re-colouring the graphics.

Inserting Clip Art in a Slide

1. Add a new Title Only slide

2. Select `Insert`, `Clip Art`, the Insert Clip Art dialog box appears

Figure 58

3. In the Search for: box type, Business, press `Go`

4. The Insert Clip Art dialog box shows the results

5. Click on the ▼ arrow on the picture, select `Insert`

Figure 59

6. The picture is displayed in the slide

7. Drag with the left ↲ button to reposition the picture within the slide

8. To delete the picture, click in the picture with the left ↲ button, press Delete

Edit a Picture in a Slide

1. Click on the picture

Figure 60

2. Move the mouse pointer ⬉ over the sizing handles

3. Drag to edit the picture

4. To move the picture to another position, click in the picture and drag

5. To rotate the picture, click in the picture, the Picture Tools Tab appears

6. Select Rotate ▣▾ from the Format Arrange Grouping

7. Move the mouse pointer ⬉ over the options to see how the picture will look

Figure 61

8. Select ◢ Flip Horizontal

9. Move the mouse pointer ⬉ to a green circle ⊙, a black circular arrow appears

10. Click and hold down the left 🖰 button, drag to rotate to the required position

Figure 62

Cropping Pictures

The Picture Tools option appears when a picture is selected in a slide.

1. Click the left ⌖ button on the picture

Figure 63

2. Click on from the Picture Tools

Figure 64

3. Move over a black handle

4. Press the left ⌖ button and drag to hide the information not required

5. Repeat the process until you see the tigers face

Figure 65

6. To alter the size of the picture select [Format]

Figure 66

7. Click the arrows in the height and width area from the Size Grouping

8. To expand the Size Grouping click on downward pointing arrow 🔲

9. The Size and Position dialog box appear

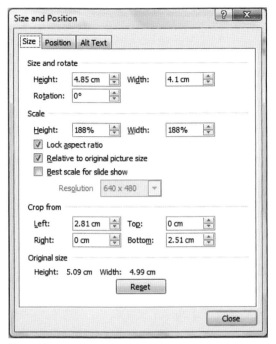

Figure 67

10. In the Scale area, amend the **H**eight and **W**idth to 300%

11. Click ⌧ Close

Inserting WordArt into a Document

1. To insert text as an object, select `Insert`,

2. The WordArt Gallery appears

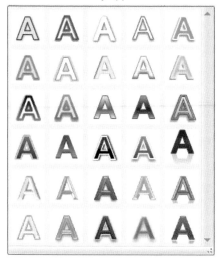

Figure 68

3. Select a style, the Edit WordArt dialog box appears in the slide

Figure 69

4. In the Text box type ABC Limited

Figure 70

5. Highlight the text, select

6. Click on 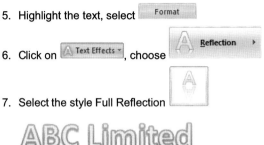, choose

7. Select the style Full Reflection

Figure 71

8. To rotate the text, highlight the text, select

9. Choose ,

10. Click with the left button on the required option in the gallery

Figure 72

Format WordArt in a Slide

1. To change the colour of the WordArt
2. Highlight the text to be changed

SMART PC GUIDES

Figure 73

3. Choose Format, select , choose the required colour

Figure 74

4. To format the WordArt, click in the WordArt to be changed

5. Click with the right button, select | Format Text Effects...

6. The Format Text Effects dialog box appears

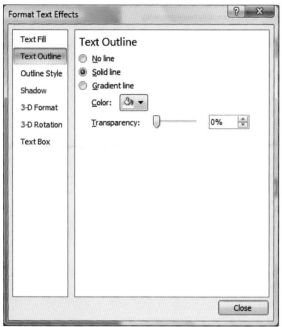

Figure 75

7. Select | Text Outline |, change the text outline colour Color:

8. To alter the layout, select | Text Box |, choose the layout required

9. Press | Close |

Adding AutoShapes to a Slide

Ready-made basic shapes - rectangles, circles, block arrows, flowcharts, symbols, banners and callouts - can be added to a slide to enhance its appearance.

1. Select  from the Illustrations Grouping

2. The Shapes gallery appears, choose Callouts

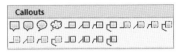

Figure 76

3. Select a shape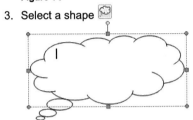

Figure 77

4. Drag in the slide for the AutoShape to appear

5. Type in the AutoShape the text required

6. The text appears in the AutoShape in the slide

Figure 78

Using the Drawing Toolbar

1. To use a drawing object, select Line 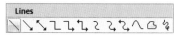 from the Shapes gallery

Figure 79

2. Hold down the left button and drag

3. Click back on the Line icon

4. Position the mouse pointer on the circle next to the line and drag

Figure 80

5. Repeat the above steps to complete the required shape

6. To draw a shape, click on the shape from the Shapes gallery

7. Move the mouse pointer where you want the object to appear

8. Hold down the left button and drag, release the mouse button

9. Repeat the process to create as many shapes as required

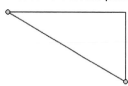

Figure 81

To Draw Objects from a Central Point

1. Select an object from the Shapes gallery with the left button
2. Press and hold down the ⌈Ctrl⌋ key, drag the object onto the slide
3. Release the mouse button before the ⌈Ctrl⌋ key
4. Click outside the drawing box

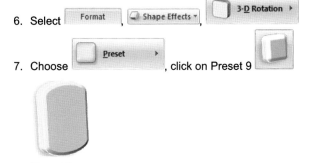

Figure 82

5. To add a 3-D effect, select the object

6. Select ⌈Format⌋ , ⌈Shape Effects ▾⌋ , ⌈3-D Rotation ▸⌋

7. Choose ⌈Preset ▸⌋ , click on Preset 9

Figure 83

To Draw A Text Box

Text boxes allow text to be positioned anywhere in a slide.

1. To insert a text box, select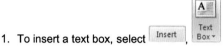

2. Click where you want to start the text box, drag to the required size

Figure 84

3. Click inside the box to add text

4. To move the text box, click on the edge of the box

5. Use the arrow keys to move to the new position

6. To delete a text box

7. Position the mouse pointer 🖑 over the edge of the text box, press Delete

Inserting Objects

1. Add a Title Slide to your presentation

2. Select

3. Click with the left 🖱 button on Create from file, choose Browse..., select the file

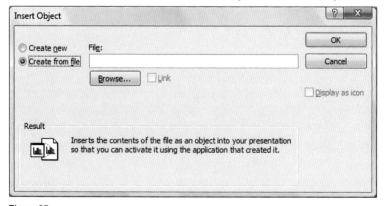

Figure 85

4. Read the Result in the screen print preview area

5. Click the link icon ☑ Link to review the revised results

6. This enables changes in the file to be reflected in the slide

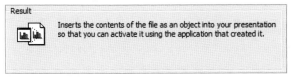

Figure 86

7. Click [OK], the object appears in the presentation

Opening a Presentation containing Linked Information

If changes have been made to a linked object when the PowerPoint file is opened, select **U**pdate Links to add the latest image of the object.

Exercise 5: - Drawing Shapes

1. Open a new presentation
2. Select a blank layout slide
3. Insert an Oval shape
4. Move the mouse pointer ⬚ into the slide a black hairline cross appears
5. Click with the left ⬚ button, the selected shape is displayed
6. Alternatively click and drag in the slide to the desired size for the shape
7. Produce the following slide

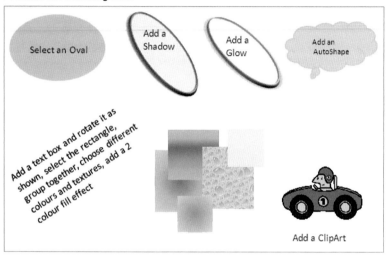

8. Save the slide

Using the Chart Layout Feature

PowerPoint allows you to create a chart or import a Microsoft Excel worksheet or chart. You can enter your own data on the datasheet, import data from a text file, or paste data from another program.

The advantage of working with the chart layout slide is that information can be presented graphically on one slide making it is easier to understand. In slide layout there are a number of different ways to display a chart, an example of the four most popular styles are displayed below:

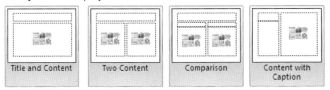

Figure 87

1. Select a new presentation, choose a slide containing a chart feature

2. Click with the left ⏻ button on the chart icon ⬚ to add the chart to the slide

3. The Insert Chart dialog box appears

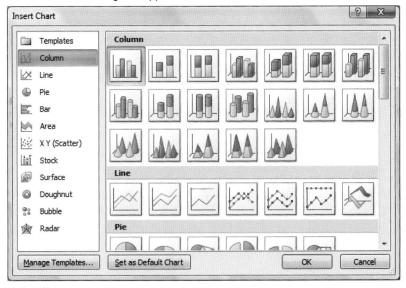

Figure 88

4. Select  ,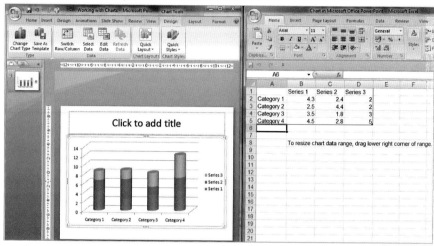

5. Click [OK]

6. The window screen splits to show the PowerPoint slide and the Excel data

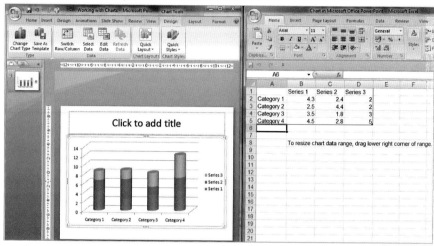

Figure 89

7. Using the Excel sheet change or update the data as required

8. Click outside the data area

9. Click into the PowerPoint slide, the chart is updated automatically

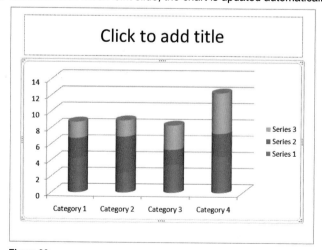

Figure 90

10. To edit the data click in the chart, select Data to bring back the Excel data sheet

11. Edit the data and close the Excel screen

12. The data is updated in the chart

13. To change the colour scheme in the chart, click in the chart area

14. Select the Design Tab, choose Colors to expand the colour gallery

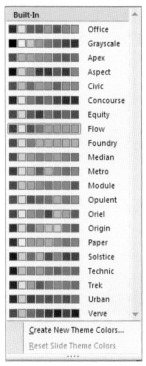

Figure 91

15. Use the mouse pointer ⟍ to hover over the different colour schemes

16. The different colour schemes are shown on the slide

17. Click to select the required colour scheme

18. To change the chart type, click in the chart area

19. Select Chart Type, the Change Chart Type dialog box appears

20. Choose 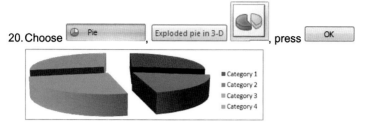, press OK

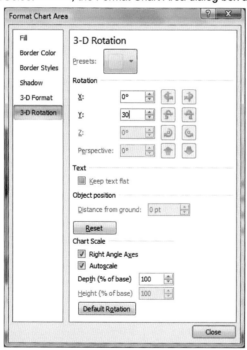

Figure 92

21. To rotate data in the chart, click in the chart area

22. Select Layout from the Chart Tools area

23. Select 3-D Rotation, the Format Chart Area dialog box appears

Figure 93

24. Use the arrows to change the rotation

25. Press Close, the slide is updated, save the presentation

Running a Slide Show

PowerPoint enables a presentation to be run through a projector as a slide show. It could, for example be used to promote a new product in the form of a presentation from a Reception area, in this example timing and transitions would be applied to the presentation to attract the attention of both staff and visitors who could view information on the new product.

Another example may require the presenter to progress to the next slide when they are ready; therefore timings would not be required in this form of delivery. In both examples the slides may contain transitions and build effects to enhance the presentation.

1. Open the presentation My First Presentation, click on the first slide

2. Choose ⟨ Slide Show ⟩, choose ⟨ From Beginning ⟩, alternatively press ⟨F5⟩

3. Click with the left 🖱 button to display the second slide

4. Repeat the process for the rest of the slides

5. Alternatively use ⟨←⟩ ⟨→⟩ ⟨↑⟩ ⟨↓⟩, press ⟨F1⟩ to learn more on Slide Show options

6. To exit Slide Show press the ⟨Esc⟩ key on the keyboard

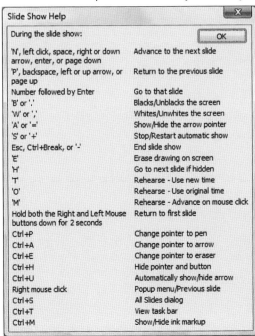

Figure 94

Hide and Unhide Slides in Slide Sorter View

Presentations can be delivered to a different audience by hiding slides that are not relevant to that audience.

1. Open a presentation, select View , Slide Sorter

2. Move the mouse pointer over the slide to be hidden

3. Click with the right button, choose Hide Slide

4. A diagonal line is displayed through the chosen slide

5. The slide will not be displayed when running a presentation using the slide show

6. To Unhide the slide move the mouse pointer over the hidden slide

7. Click with the right button, choose Hide Slide

8. The normal slide number is displayed

Applying Slide Transitions

Transition effects can be added to a presentation to enhance the visual appearance of a slide(s).

1. Select Animations

2. Click on the downward arrow from the Transition To This Slide Grouping

Figure 95

3. The gallery is expanded

4. Move the mouse pointer over the designs to see how they appear in the presentation

5. Choose the required transition

6. The default speed of the transition is automatically set to fast

7. To select a slower speed, choose Transition Speed: Fast

8. Using the downward pointing arrow select the required speed

| Slow |
| Medium |
| Fast |

9. To add sound to the transition, select  Transition Sound: [No Sound] ▾

10. Using the downward pointing arrow ▾ select the sound required

11. If the sound needs to be applied to all the slides select ⊞ Apply To All

Rehearse Timings

PowerPoint allows timings to be set in presentations.

1. Select the first slide in the slide show

2. Click on Slide Show , choose 🕤 Rehearse Timings

3. The presentation is displayed with the Rehearsal counter

Rehearsal ▾ ×
⇒ II 0:00:14 ↻ 0:00:14

Figure 96

4. The ⇒ icon when selected displays the next slide

5. The II icon is used to pause the time of the presentation

6. The 0:00:06 displays the individual slide time

7. The Repeat ↻ icon restarts the individual slide to zero seconds

8. The last information area 0:00:06 displays the combined time of all the slides

9. At the end of all the slides a prompt appears

Microsoft Office PowerPoint   ×

The total time for the slide show was 0:00:51. Do you want to keep the new slide timings to use when you view the slide show?

Yes   No

Figure 97

10. To keep the new slide timings select Yes , alternatively choose No

11. Turning off timings does not delete them.

12. Turn them back on at any time without having to recreate them by

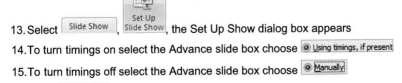

13. Select Slide Show , Slide Show , the Set Up Show dialog box appears

14. To turn timings on select the Advance slide box choose ⊙ Using timings, if present

15. To turn timings off select the Advance slide box choose ⊙ Manually

16. Press OK to return to the presentation

Shortcut Keys

SHORTCUT KEYS	DESCRIPTION	SHORTCUT KEYS	DESCRIPTION
Ctrl F1	Display or Hide the Ribbon	Alt F P	Displays Print Dialog Box
Ctrl B	Apply or Remove Bold Format	Alt H I	New Slide Options
Ctrl C	Copy Selected Information	Alt V I	Grid and Guides Dialog Box
Ctrl P	Displays Print Dialog Box	Alt W M	Slide Master Options
Ctrl S	Saves the Presentation	Alt W R	Display or Hide the Ruler
Ctrl U	Apply or Remove Underline		
Ctrl V	Paste Selected Information		
Ctrl X	Cuts Selected Information		
Ctrl Y	Repeats Previous Command		
Ctrl Z	Undo Previous Command		
Ctrl Shift P	Displays Font Dialog Box		
Ctrl F2	Displays Print Preview		
Shift F3	Upper, Lower or Initial Caps		
F1	PowerPoint Help		
F5	Starts Slide Show		
F7	Spell Checker		
F12	Save As Dialog Box		

This concludes the PowerPoint 2007 Foundation to Intermediate Guide. Thank you for choosing Smart PC Guides, we look forward to your continued use of Smart PC Guides. For a comprehensive view of our guides please visit our website www.smart-pc-guides.com

Notes Pages

Index